The Sage Who Dared to Change the World
Sreenarayana Guru

The Sage Who Dared to Change the Word
Sreenarayana Guru

M K Sanoo

Translation and Adaptation
Tensingh Kesavan

OPEN DOOR MEDIA
www.opendoormedia.in

The Sage Who Dared to Change the World

Original (Malayalam)
Kuttikalude Sree Narayana Guru
(Biography)
Author: M K Sanoo
Translation and adaptation: Tensingh Kesavan

Publishing:
Open Door Media
7/259 PSBP Tower Vikasvani
Thengode P O, Kakkanad
Kochi 682030 India.

E mail: tensingh@opendoormedia.in
www.opendoormedia.in
Customer care: +91 8547854006

Publishing year: August 2025

Page layout: Rishy Vettoor

Printed at:

ISBN:978-81-942620-4-6

Rs. 200.00

Dedication

To the visionaries who participated in the historic All Religions Conference of 1924, held at the Advaita Ashram in Aluva, at the behest of Sreenarayana Guru — the first such gathering in India to promote interfaith harmony.

With special remembrance of my father, Vadakkeparampil Kesavan Vaidyar of Kanjippadom, Ambalappuzha, who was one among them.

Tensingh Kesavan

About the Author

Prof. M. K. Sanoo (b. 27 October 1927) is one of the most respected and influential literary figures in Malayalam. A distinguished writer, critic, educator, orator, and social activist, his contributions over the past seven decades have left a lasting imprint on Kerala's cultural and intellectual life. He began his academic career as a lecturer at Sree Narayana College and Maharaja's College, and went on to author over sixty books, including biographies, literary criticism, translations, and essays. His writings are known for their intellectual depth, moral clarity, and commitment to justice and human dignity.

Renowned for his eloquence and persuasive public speaking, Prof. Sanoo has inspired generations through both his teaching and oratory. A tireless advocate for social justice, he has been especially vocal in defending the rights of marginalized communities. He is a permanent member of the International Body for Human Rights and currently serves as Chief Editor of Sahodaran, the historic magazine founded by Sahodaran Ayyappan in 1917. Prof. Sanoo served as a Member of the Kerala Legislative Assembly (1987–1991), was President of the Kerala Sahitya Academy (1988–1991), and also led the Kerala Progressive Writers' Union.

Selected Honours and Awards

Kerala Sahitya Academy Award for - Literary Criticism (1985)

Vayalar Award (1992)

Kendra Sahitya Academy Award for Basheer: Ekantha Veedhiyile Avadhoothan (2011)

Abu Dhabi Sakthi Awards (2011, 2013, 2020)
Ezhuthachan Puraskaram – Kerala's highest literary honour (2013)
Father Vadakkan Puraskaram (2014)
P. Kesavadev Literary Award (2015)
Chavara Samskruthy Puraskaram (2021)
Honorary D.Litt. – Mahatma Gandhi University (2022) and Sree Sankaracharya University of Sanskrit
Sree Narayana Sahitya Kulapathy Award (2023)
Kerala Jyothi – the state's highest civilian honour (2024)

About the Translator

Tensingh Kesavan is a publishing and print-production professional with over 40 years of experience, including a long career in advertising and book publishing in India and abroad. He now heads Open Door Media, a Publishing House.

He comes from a family devoted to Sreenarayana Guru—his father, Vadakkeparampil Kesavan Vaidyar, participated in the historic 1923 All Religions' Conference at Adwaithasramam in Aluva. His mother, Sarojam, took part in early Panthibhojanam events.

Tensingh is a Patron of Sree Narayana Mandira Samiti, Mumbai.

This translation and adaptation of 'Kuttikalude Sreenarayana Guru', titled Sage Who Dared to Change the World: Sree Narayana Guru - A Concise Biography for Young Adults and Beyond, is his tribute to the Guru and a gift to future generation.

Contents

Forword

In the vast tapestry of history, certain figures emerge whose wisdom and unwavering resolve fundamentally alter the course of society. Among these luminous individuals, Sreenarayana Guru stands as a titan. Born into a Kerala suffocated by the rigid shackles of the caste system, where human beings were cruelly fragmented by artificial distinctions, his very existence became a beacon piercing the pervasive darkness of prejudice and ignorance. This book invites you on a profound journey through his extraordinary life, commencing with the audacious act that shattered centuries of oppression: the consecration of the Shivalinga at Aruvippuram. This single, powerful declaration reverberated with the undeniable truth of humanity's inherent equality.

From his early years, where his innate compassion and brilliant intellect shone brightly as Nanu, to his relentless pursuit of truth as a wandering ascetic, he evolved into Sreenarayana Guru, a visionary spiritual master. He not only envisioned but tirelessly labored for a world where humanity is one family — a truly revolutionary concept in a society torn apart by the brutal practices of untouchability and discrimination.

This narrative meticulously explores his formative years, his rigorous spiritual discipline at Maruthwamala culminating in profound enlightenment, and his courageous return to society. He returned armed not with anger, but with the boundless power of universal love and wisdom. The book reveals how he systematically dismantled superstitious beliefs, redefined the very essence of true religion, and established groundbreaking organizations like the SNDP Yogam. These institutions were designed to empower the downtrodden through the transformative forces of education, unity, and self-respect.

The Guru's teachings, simple yet profoundly impactful, championed inner purity, ethical living, and the recognition of the Divine within every individual. He unequivocally demonstrated that genuine worship lay in serving humanity and that spiritual liberation was inextricably intertwined with social justice. This compelling work illuminates his transformative journey, his unwavering commitment to human dignity, and the enduring legacy of his "Beams of Dharma." These timeless principles continue to inspire millions, guiding them along the path of unity, love, and enlightenment, and paving the way for a more harmonious world.

This remarkable account is translated and adapted from Prof. M.K. Sanoo's acclaimed Malayalam work, Kuttikalude Sreenarayana Guru (Sreenarayana Guru for Children). Tensingh Kesavan, the translator, has not merely provided a literal rendering; rather, he has skillfully adapted and expanded upon the original text, ensuring that the core essence and profound message of Guru's life resonate deeply with readers while remaining true to Prof. Sanoo's insightful portrayal. This book serves as an excellent resource for young adults and beyond, offering a compelling introduction to a towering figure whose relevance only grows with time.

Navi Mumbai,
July 02, 2025

M I Damodaran
President
Sree Narayana Mandira Samiti
Mumbai.

Preface

When I began the journey of 'translating Kuttikalude Sreenarayana Guru', I knew it was more than just a translation of words; it was about carrying a light. Sreenarayana Guru's life offers both history and inspiration. Each chapter reveals not only the events of his life but also the timeless values he lived by. Sage Who Dared to Change the World is an adaptation of Prof. M.K. Sanoo's original Malayalam book, Kuttikalude Sreenarayana Guru (Sree Narayana Guru for Children), rather than a word-for-word translation. We've aimed to preserve the lyrical simplicity and moral clarity of the original Malayalam text, while making the language accessible to children, young adults, and readers across the English-speaking world. This book is designed for classrooms, libraries, and homes — anywhere a child opens a book in search of truth, courage, and compassion. I thank the original author, Prof. M.K. Sanoo and the visionaries who made this translation possible.

Tensingh Kesavan

1

The Foundation of A Vision

The year was 1888. On the sacred day of Shivaratri, a profound anticipation vibrated through the very air, drawing people from countless tiny hamlets and scattered homesteads towards a single, holy destination. Winding village paths, still dusty and unpaved, often mere foot-trodden tracks through fields and scrubland, buzzed with a singular, purposeful movement. Streams of men, women, and children, predominantly from modest homes of labourers and farmers, but with a sprinkling from the middle class of small landowners, local merchants, and skilled artisans, walked with spirited resolve. They left behind the familiar comforts of their simple dwellings, turning their faces resolutely northwest, towards a secluded spot nestled deep within the verdant landscape, some 24 kilometres from Trivandrum, then a distant, burgeoning town, the seat of the Maharaja's rule.

The long, arduous paths were softened by the presence of tall, verdant trees, their wide leaves forming natural canopies that offered a cool, welcome relief from the relentless sun and the weariness of the journey. Here and there, walkers paused by the welcome sight of bubbling springs, the clear water a precious gift. Some cupped their hands, gratefully drinking the sweet, cold water, while others splashed it over their faces and feet, washing away the dust and fatigue. At intervals, compassionate souls, often villagers themselves, had set up humble stalls beneath makeshift palm-leaf roofs, freely offering simple food and refreshing drinks to the weary travellers. As they rested and sipped, a quiet murmur ran through the throngs. Pilgrims spoke in low, hopeful voices, their hearts swelling with faith: "Today we will have darshan of Swami. Today we will surely receive his blessings." In their hearts, they truly believed that his sacred presence, a mere glimpse, would bring peace and solutions to their most pressing troubles.

Their collective destination was Aruvippuram, a tranquil spot nestled amidst nature's embrace. People were arriving from all directions, following countless different footpaths and tracks, yet all drawn by the same profound purpose. While the Shivaratri celebration lent an undeniable energy to the atmosphere, the true, magnetic force was a young ascetic – a spiritual figure whose quiet power had profoundly captured the people's imagination. Tales of his intense penance and miraculous deeds had spread far and wide, whispered from hearth to hearth. It was said he possessed the ability to tame evil spirits, cure chronic sicknesses, and bring abundant blessings to those who sought him with earnest hearts. And alongside these wondrous stories, it was softly whispered that he spoke gently to the common folk, urging them to think for themselves, to question deeply ingrained and often harmful customs, and to shed the weight of superstitions.

After years of solitary meditation, a period of profound self-realization, he had come to Aruvippuram, carrying with him a deep, almost palpable spiritual force. His eyes were strikingly calm, brimming with an expansive compassion, and radiated a profound peace that seemed to touch and soothe everyone he met. His very presence commanded an instinctive reverence, silent yet powerful, like a golden idol shimmering with an inner light. It was for this reason that so many were eager to gather here on this holy night – because he had called them, a rare and momentous invitation. They respectfully referred to him as "Swami," a title denoting profound spiritual respect, though those closest to him affectionately called him Nanuswami. Even if direct conversation or personal interaction was not possible, a mere glimpse of him was considered a rare and transformative blessing, a moment to be cherished.

From every direction, the streams of devotees continued to converge at Aruvippuram. Between two gentle, verdant hills, a cheerful stream, a lively tributary of the larger Neyyar River, flowed gracefully, its crystal-clear water seemingly 'laughing' as it danced and babbled over smooth, river-worn stones. The perpetual sound was like a soft, rhythmic chant, a never-ending prayer echoing through the valley. In this serene place, embraced by thick, untamed greenery, there was a small, unassuming cave, just large enough for one person to sit comfortably. Inside it sat Swami, lost in the profound depths of deep meditation. Devotees gathered reverently around the mouth of the cave; some, bolder or more desperate, approached him with quiet questions, while others simply stand nearby, hands folded in respectful Anjali mudra, gazing at him in silent awe.

The temple grounds, though simple, were being meticulously decorated with vibrant, colourful garlands woven from fresh flowers and leaves. As the tropical darkness began its slow encroachment, oil lamps began to glow softly, one by one, dotting the landscape with warm, flickering lights. Musicians, having travelled far, carefully tuned their traditional instruments, preparing for the sacred night of chanting and devotion ahead. This particular night's festival was unique for two profound reasons: first, Swami himself had personally invited the people to come – an unprecedented gesture; and second, Swami is about to perform the consecration of the temple – a sacred duty traditionally and rigidly reserved only for Brahmins, the priestly class. However, Swami is from the Ezhava community, a group long subjected to severe social exclusion and historically forbidden from such sacred roles. His audacious action would mark a profound rupture in Kerala's deeply entrenched and oppressive caste tradition.

As midnight arrived, casting long, dancing shadows, the simple temple and its surrounding grounds shimmered under the ethereal light of hundreds of tiny, glowing oil lamps. From the quiet depths of the cave, Swami emerged, serene and composed, his movements unhurried. The waiting crowd, a sea of expectant faces, respectfully made way for him, parting in silent deference. With deliberate, graceful steps, he walked into the cold, clear stream, its waters a gentle embrace. After dipping into the refreshing current, he emerged, his hand gently holding a stone – it is a Shivalinga, a symbolic representation of the deity Shiva. A collective gasp, soft and reverent, rippled through the crowd, and instinctively, thousands of hands rose and folded in prayer. Swami walked to the temple pavilion and resumed his meditation, sitting perfectly still for nearly three hours, an unwavering pillar of spiritual focus. All around him, devotees began to chant the panchaksharee mantra, 'Om Namah Shivaya,' their voices rising and falling in a rhythmic wave of devotion, many eyes moist with tears of profound faith and anticipation.

Around 3 a.m., as the world seemed to hold its breath, Swami opened his eyes. Under the vast, star-dusted sky, as nature itself seemed to stand in reverent stillness, he installed the Shivalinga on the specially prepared pedestal. This exact moment was not chosen for any complex astrological significance, nor did anyone consult ancient almanacs. Yet, in the unfolding pages of Kerala's rich and complex history, this single, quiet act would shine forever as the incandescent beginning of a spiritual and social revolution. A non-Brahmin had consecrated a temple, an act that shook centuries of rigid, unjust tradition in a single, powerful act of silent defiance. When a learned scholar, perhaps bewildered or outraged by this transgression, protested, daring to ask Swami what right he, an Ezhava, had to perform this sacred ritual, Swami replied calmly but with an unwavering, firm conviction: "We only installed the 'Ezhava Shiva'." His words, simple yet profound, resonated with a power that promised to reshape destinities.

2

The Blessing of Chempazhanthi

Chapter One detailed the historic consecration of the Shivalinga at Aruvippuram, a moment of profound spiritual defiance performed by Swami himself on the sacred day of Shivaratri in the Malayalam month of Kumbham, 1063 ME (February 1888 CE). At that pivotal time, Swami was thirty-two years old, a figure of serene power. To truly grasp the seismic significance of that spiritual revolution, one must journey back further, deep into the very origins of the man who would be revered as Sreenarayana Guru – to the quiet dawn of his early life.

Swami was born in the serene and relatively secluded village of Chempazhanthi, nestled approximately six kilometres, north of Thiruvananthapuram. In those days, the landscape of Chempazhanthi was a tapestry of vast, shimmering paddy fields and dense, ancient forests. These wild, verdant expanses teemed with an abundance of wildlife – deer, wild boar, and various fowl – making them favoured hunting grounds for the local aristocracy, the few who held power and privilege. It was in this picturesque and lush environment, beside the life-giving expanse of a paddy field, that

Narayanan – later revered as Sreenarayana Guru – was born under the Chathayam star in the Malayalam month of Chingam, 1032 ME (August–September 1856 CE).

His birthplace was a modest yet deeply respected home known throughout the village as Vayalvarathu Veedu, a name that literally translated to "the house beside the paddy fields." Although the family belonged to the Ezhava community, which was tragically considered socially 'lower' and was subjected to severe discrimination at the time, Vayalvarathu Veedu held an unusually high regard within Chempazhanthi. This respect, rare for their caste, was not derived from inherited material wealth, for they possessed little, nor from any caste privilege, for they had none. Instead, it stemmed from the profound integrity, keen intellect, and inherent spiritual depth of its members, qualities that commanded respect from all who encountered them.

Narayanan's father, Madan Asan, was more than just a village teacher; he was a respected local scholar with a good understanding of basic Sanskrit, a language of profound learning traditionally restricted to upper castes. His gentle wisdom made him a beacon of knowledge in the community. His mother, Kutti, possessed a strong foundation in the Puranas, ancient Hindu scriptures filled with myths and legends, which she diligently studied and recited daily, filling their home with a sacred resonance. However, the most influential figure in shaping young Narayanan's precocious intellectual path was his maternal uncle, Krishnan Vaidyar. He was a highly respected Ayurvedic physician (Vaidyan), whose profound knowledge of traditional medicine and intricate Sanskrit scholarship transcended the rigid social barriers. Despite the oppressive caste structure of society, even upper-caste families, in their desperate need for healing, sought his medical expertise and wise counsel, acknowledging the undeniable depth of his knowledge and remarkable healing skills. It is important to note that Kerala, during that era, uniquely followed a matrilineal system, and it was Krishnan Vaidyar who played a singularly active role in guiding and nurturing Narayanan's early learning, recognizing the exceptional spark within the boy.

Further adding to the family's quietly spiritual eminence was Kochan Asan, Kutti's maternal uncle. A celibate and ascetic scholar of great renown, Kochan Asan was a beacon of wisdom, purity, and unwavering devotion, known and respected by people of all castes, even those who might otherwise practice social exclusion. His life of simplicity, profound contemplation, and unshakeable devotion made him, in many ways, the spiritual soul of Chempazhanthi, a living embodiment of goodness. This unique and powerful blend of scholarship, deep spiritual inclination, and an inherent social conscience bestowed a quiet yet profound influence upon Vayalvarathu Veedu. Though situated firmly within the boundaries of a marginalized community, this home exuded an undeniable dignity and depth of character, silently commanding respect from all who knew its inhabitants.

Yet, the world into which Narayanan was born was not merely challenging; it was profoundly riddled with an entrenched, brutal injustice. Kerala's society at the time was rigidly stratified into an unforgiving system of castes, with the Brahmins firmly positioned at the apex, wielding immense power and privilege. Below them, the so-called 'lower' castes, including the Ezhavas and many others, were brutally confined to the very margins of society, stripped of their basic human dignity. People from these oppressed communities faced daily, soul-crushing indignities: they were systematically not allowed to enter temples, forbidden from attending schools, or even permitted to walk freely on public pathways designated for upper castes. The mere shadow of a lower-caste person was believed, under this abhorrent system, to cause 'pollution' to an upper-caste individual, who would then be forced to bathe and purify themselves in elaborate rituals. This abominable practice of untouchability, in all its cruel manifestations, was locally known as Ayitham or Theendal. The oppression was not just physical, limiting movement and access – it was deeply psychological and spiritual, insidious in its power, forcing people to internalize a belief in their own inherent inferiority. Caste, in this land, was employed as a brutal and effective tool to construct invisible yet impenetrable walls between human beings, denying shared humanity. Even the pure and noble idea of God, meant to unite and uplift, became tragically entangled in this cruel, man-made hierarchy. Religion, which should have been a unifying force of compassion, was instead wielded with devastating effect to divide and dehumanize.

The renowned poet Kumaran Asan, one of Swami's most devoted disciples and a powerful voice against social injustice, later expressed the profound horror of this world in a poignant and powerful lament: "Even seeing a fellow human is said to cause defilement here. Alas! What a hell this land is!" His sorrowful words echoed the pain and anguish of countless others who lived under the crushing, dehumanizing weight of this oppressive system.

Into this deeply fractured society, into this crucible of injustice, Narayanan was born — a child of quiet promise, raised in a home steeped in learning, compassion, and unwavering moral strength. Though born into the Ezhava community, a group systematically denied dignity and basic rights, he would grow up to become the very force that questioned, challenged, and ultimately transformed this oppressive order. The initial spark of revolution had been lit in the humble village of Chempazhanthi, nurtured in Vayalvarathu Veedu, and in the chapters ahead, we will witness how that nascent flame grew steadily, inexorably, into a roaring fire that could not be contained, illuminating a path to a more just and equitable world.

3

The Nature of Purity

It was Nanu's beloved maternal uncle, Krishnan Vaidyar, the esteemed Ayurvedic physician and scholar, who gave him his name. He was called Narayanan, a name that soon softened into the affectionate and universally familiar form of Nanu within the village of Chempazhanthi. Like most children of his era, Nanu's early years were filled with simple, earthy joys — the feel of warm dust between his toes, the thrill of playing beneath the generous shade of ancient trees, the quiet satisfaction of learning to read and write on palm leaves. But from a remarkably young age, those closest to him began to notice something rare, an almost other-worldly quality about this child: an unusually serene presence and a mind that seemed far older, far more contemplative, than his tender years.

At the tender age of five, in keeping with cherished village custom, Nanu underwent Vidyarambham — the ceremonial initiation into learning. This was not a grand affair, but a humble yet sacred rite that marked his formal entry into the world of letters. He was enrolled at a nearby village school, a simple structure with a thatched roof, its floor of packed earth, where local children gathered to learn the basics of language, numbers, and sacred scripture. It didn't take long for his teachers to notice his startling brilliance. While other students grappled slowly with their lessons, their minds wrestling with new concepts, Nanu absorbed knowledge with astonishing ease, as if it were simply flowing into him. His clarity of thought, razor-sharp memory, and remarkably quick comprehension made him stand out unmistakably, like a lone, brightly blooming flower in a field. Soon, he had far outpaced his classmates. The village teacher, a man of simple means but keen observation, began to give Nanu individual attention, not out of favouritism, but out of sheer necessity—Nanu was advancing far beyond the standard curriculum.

He was not just bright; he was voraciously hungry to learn, driven by an insatiable curiosity. At home, he devoured every book within reach: the rich narratives of the Puranas, the timeless wisdom of the epics, the lyrical beauty of classic poems, intricate medical treatises, and profound spiritual texts. The house, Vayalvarathu Veedu, thanks to its lineage of scholars and spiritual seekers, had a small but surprisingly rich library, and Nanu moved through it like a tireless seeker drawn to an inexhaustible well of truth. He began studying Sanskrit with meticulous care, his young mind delighting in its intricate grammar and profound philosophy. By his early teenage years, he had acquired a remarkable mastery over both Malayalam, his native tongue, and Sanskrit. Eventually, his intellectual reach extended further; he would also learn Tamil, immersing himself in its classic literature with admiration and deep insight.

Yet what truly set Nanu apart, far more than his prodigious intellect, was the extraordinary nature of his heart. He was filled with an exceptional sense of empathy—a deep, instinctive karuna, or compassion, that extended its gentle touch to every living being, great or small. Unlike many children, who might thoughtlessly chase dragonflies or capture butterflies out of idle amusement, Nanu would intervene gently, his voice soft yet firm, asking his playmates to set the delicate creatures free. "Poor things," he would say, his brow furrowed with concern, "They too must have the right to fly, to live, to enjoy the world as we do." His voice, simple and utterly sincere, possessed a curious, compelling power — it moved others, stirring something deep within them. Even his boisterous friends, caught in the thoughtless momentum of play, would pause and listen, their hands dropping their captive prey.

Two incidents from his childhood, recounted with reverence by those who knew him, vividly reveal the remarkable depth of his compassion. Once, some boys, in their youthful ignorance, had cruelly caught a baby pigeon. One of its fragile wings had already been clipped; they were preparing, with grim intent, to cut the other. Nanu arrived just in time, his heart seizing with horror. He took the frightened, trembling bird gently into his arms, his luminous eyes brimming with unshed tears. "Why did you do this? Would it feel good if someone cut your hand or foot? This little bird is alive—just like us." The boys, struck silent by the sheer purity and earnestness of his plea, lowered their eyes in shame, unable to meet his gaze. Nanu carried the injured bird home, tending to it with the most tender care and unwavering patience until its wing miraculously healed. And one glorious day, with deep joy swelling in his heart, he released it into the wide, boundless sky, watching it soar towards freedom.

On another occasion, a wandering sanyasi, a renunciate draped in faded saffron robes, his hair wild and matted, was passing through the village. The local children, frightened by his strange, unkempt appearance, began mocking him, their fear quickly turning into aggression as they threw stones and mud. The frightened sanyasi tried desperately to flee, but the relentless children pursued him. Suddenly, Nanu appeared, seemingly from nowhere, placing his slight frame squarely between the unruly crowd and the terrified ascetic. "By the name of God, do not harm this swami," he said, his young voice steady and full of unshakeable conviction, echoing with a quiet authority. "If you must throw stones, throw them at me instead." The children stopped dead in their tracks, their arms lowered. No one dared challenge Nanu—not out of fear of physical retribution, but out of an inexplicable, deep-seated respect for his moral courage. His calm, resolute presence diffused the tension, quieting even the most unruly and boisterous among them.

Physically too, Nanu carried a quiet, almost regal grace. His skin had a warm, golden glow, his limbs were perfectly proportioned and carried a natural strength, his eyes were luminous with inner thought, and his forehead was broad and contemplative, hinting at the vastness of his mind. He rarely needed to raise his voice or assert himself aggressively. His mere presence—calm, alert, and quietly radiant—made people pause, listen, and reflect.

One day, Nanu returned from school with tell-tale soot and charcoal stains smudged on his hands and clothes. His mother, Kutti, ever observant, immediately asked what had happened. He explained, without a hint of hesitation or perceived transgression, that he had seen a pot of boiling gruel spilling over in a nearby Pulaya hut. Without a moment's thought for social strictures or personal consequence, he had run in and, using his bare hands, bravely lifted the dangerously hot vessel off the fire to prevent the family's meagre meal from being lost entirely. His mother, though herself a kind-hearted soul, was deeply bound by the rigid caste beliefs of the time. "Did you enter a Pulaya hut? Don't you know that makes you impure?" she asked, her voice laced with distress and concern for her son's ritual purity. But Nanu responded gently, his innocence cutting through centuries of prejudice: "If I hadn't helped, the family would have gone hungry, Amma. How can helping them be a sin? Would God really ask us to turn away when someone is suffering and in need?" Her heart, caught between rigid tradition and her son's pure logic, melted. She could not argue with such unassailable innocence and fundamental truth.

Soon, Nanu began to visit the homes of Pulaya families without hesitation, a truly radical act in that era. He would talk to them, hold their hands, and offer them kindness and solidarity, defying all prevailing norms of untouchability. If they tried to run away from him—afraid of punishment for their perceived 'pollution' or fearful of bringing harm upon him—he would gently but firmly stop them and ask, his voice resonating with simple truth, "Are we not all human? Why should you run from me?" These actions were not merely unconventional; in a world dominated by invisible yet brutal barriers of caste and forbidden touch, such behaviour was utterly shocking—even overtly subversive. But no one, not even the most conservative villagers, could bring themselves to scold Nanu. His transparent sincerity, his innate goodness, disarmed even the most hardened hearts and rigid minds. By now, everyone in the village knew of the remarkable boy who was wise beyond his years, who lived by a higher code. He had become a gentle but powerful presence—a child who challenged prejudice not with anger or confrontation, but with the quiet, undeniable force of truth and compassion.

There was yet another profound dimension to Nanu that set him apart—his deep thoughtfulness and an almost magnetic, natural pull toward meditation. All people think, but some rare souls are drawn to profound reflection as if it were the very breath of life itself, a vital sustenance. Nanu was such a soul. He constantly questioned what others took for granted, delving into the mysteries of existence. Once, he disappeared for hours. Alarmed, his family, fearing the wild animals of the surrounding forests or some other peril, searched everywhere with growing panic. They finally found him sitting quietly by a stream, hidden in the dappled shade of a dense forest grove, utterly lost in profound thought. When asked why he had gone there, his simple reply was deeply philosophical: "I saw people crying bitterly when someone died, and then laughing and living joyfully a few days later as if nothing had happened. I came here to understand—what is death? What is this strange world we live in where such contradictions exist?" His father, Madan Asan, would often shake his head, half in pride and half in genuine worry, muttering, "I don't know what this boy will grow up to be. He thinks thoughts that don't belong to ordinary people." Indeed, Nanu was not ordinary. He was quietly, yet resolutely, beginning to walk a path entirely his own—one carved not by the rigid confines of caste or the expectations of convention, but by the silent, profound calling of his soul, destined for a greater purpose.

4

On the Path of Knowledge

Let us now step into the bustling market street of Chala in Thiruvananthapuram. Inside a busy provision shop, beside a man meticulously writing accounts, sits a young boy—approximately fifteen years old. His face glows with an almost heavenly innocence and serene calmness. In his hands, he holds a book, which he reads with an intensity of focus that belies his age. Occasionally, the accountant, recognizing his acumen, asks him a question. The boy listens attentively and replies with thoughtful precision. This boy, radiating quiet wisdom, is Nanu.

How did Nanu come to be here, in the vibrant heart of Chala? He frequently travelled to visit relatives in both Thiruvananthapuram and Neyyattinkara. These journeys were not merely for familial connection—though he cherished his loved ones—but were stirred by an inner urge to wander, to observe, and above all, to learn. He moved freely from one home to another, and often found refuge in temples and sacred spaces. His family, recognising his purity and quiet determination, never attempted to restrain him. They believed deeply in the promise of his unique destiny.

During one such journey, Nanu fell gravely ill with smallpox. He found shelter in a temple, where he slowly recovered in the silent company of the divine. When he returned home, the pockmarks on his face told the story. His concerned family asked, "Who took care of you?" Nanu replied simply, "When the goddess herself is there, why do we need anyone else?"

It was on another of these formative journeys that he arrived in Chala. There, he formed a close bond with a devout and learned accountant who introduced him to Tamil. With the man's generous support, Nanu began learning the language and soon attained remarkable fluency. This opened the door to the vast treasures of Tamil literature. Later in life, he would undertake the translation of the revered Thirukkural into Malayalam and even compose original Tamil poetry—testament to his deep command over languages.

While this was unfolding, he also continued his advanced studies in Sanskrit under a respected teacher back in Chempazhanthi. By the age of sixteen, Nanu had mastered both Sanskrit and Malayalam to such an extraordinary degree that even his maternal uncle, the illustrious physician and Sanskrit scholar Krishnan Vaidyar, began seeking his help with interpreting complex verses. Such was Nanu's scholarly brilliance.

Yet for Nanu, learning extended far beyond the confines of books. He believed that true knowledge sprang from experience—from travel, from visits to sacred places, from deep, reflective reading, and from sincere prayer. His idea of education was not a passive collection of information but a dynamic journey toward universal truth.

Years later, at the Aluva Advaita Ashram, Swami would reflect—half in jest, half in gravity—on the inadequacies of the modern education system. A man with a university degree in Philosophy once visited him, expecting to engage in deep discussions. Swami asked him a few basic questions about life and its essence. The man, caught off guard, began quoting Plato, Descartes, and Shankaracharya—but failed to answer from lived experience.

With a gentle smile, Swami remarked on the system's flaw. He said, "Education today is like making 'puttu'." Then, with characteristic wit, he explained: "You place layers of rice flour and grated coconut in a hollow cylindrical steamer. Steam is applied, and then you push the puttu out with a stick. The cylinder becomes hollow again. That's what happens in schools—each class adds a layer of facts and formulas. Then comes the steam—exams. The student produces results, but the mind remains empty, hollow of true wisdom."

Such was Swami's sharp yet affectionate critique—his reminder that education must nourish the soul, not just train the memory.

After completing his initial education at Chempazhanthi, Nanu enrolled in the school of the esteemed Sanskrit scholar Komampalli Raman Pillai Asan in Karunagappally. During this period, he resided with the Varanappally family. He lived as a model student—disciplined, devoted, immersed in study and meditation. He frequently visited temples, read scriptures, and always extended kindness to those in need, especially the poor and so-called 'lower-castes'. His principles were not merely spoken but lived, even amidst rigorous learning.

Later in life, Swami would often say, "A person's greatness lies in being a companion to the poor and suffering. They are the ones who truly need a friend."

Even in his youth, Nanu's heart beat for the suffering and the marginalised. Amidst studies and solitude, he must have pondered: How can I bring real comfort to those in pain? How can I uplift lives condemned to indignity?

These silent, compassionate reflections would later guide the path of his entire life.

5

The End of a Quest

Now, let us turn our attention to Maruthwamala—a small, enigmatic hill rising sharply near Nagercoil, in what is now the southernmost part of Tamil Nadu. If one were to visit the place today, they would observe rocky outcrops, ancient and weathered, standing largely bare against the sky. But in the days of our story, in the late 19th century, the hill and its entire surroundings were swathed in thick, pristine forest. Tall, ancient trees, dense shrubs with gnarled roots, and tiny, potent medicinal plants thrived in the cool, misty climate that perpetually clung to its slopes. It was a place imbued with a profound silence, broken only by the whispers of the wind and the rustle of leaves, a true haven for deep contemplation and spiritual energy.

On the very summit of this sacred hill lies a naturally flat rocky area known locally as Pillathadam, meaning 'children's footprint,' though its origins were far more ancient and mysterious. Next to it, almost hidden by verdant growth, is a small, unassuming cave. If you were to peer into the quiet depths of that cave, your eyes would be met with the extraordinary sight of a figure, radiating a subtle glow like polished gold, seated in profound, unwavering meditation. That figure was Nanu. But he was no longer merely the brilliant student and compassionate young teacher we encountered in earlier chapters. He had undergone a truly profound transformation. From a seeker of worldly knowledge, he had now fully embraced the path of a wandering monk, shedding all earthly attachments to embrace a higher, solitary calling. Now, he was revered and known throughout the region as Nanuswami.

How did this profound, almost alchemical transformation happen within his being? The answer lies in the subtle, often mysterious workings of destiny. Just as some individuals are born with an innate, undeniable gift for poetry, art, or music, a few rare souls are born with an unquenchable, burning thirst for spiritual truth, a longing that cannot be satisfied by anything mundane. Not everyone who dons saffron robes is a true monk; many merely adopt the outward symbols and superficial customs. But those who genuinely renounce everything—wealth, family, societal expectations, personal desires—and dedicate their entire lives, every breath, to the relentless pursuit of ultimate truth, they are the real sannyasis, the true renunciates. Nanuswami was, without a shadow of a doubt, one of them, a soul unmistakably destined for spiritual greatness and world-changing impact.

After completing his intense studies at Karunagappally, Nanu briefly took on the role of a teacher. During this period, people respectfully referred to him as Nanu Asan, acknowledging not just his profound knowledge but also his innate abilities to impart wisdom and guide others. Yet, he found he could not remain tied to that conventional role, however noble. A deep, persistent restlessness stirred within his heart—a yearning he couldn't ignore, a profound spiritual unease that beckoned him relentlessly towards a solitary path of self-discovery. Some poignant poems written by him during this very period eloquently express the intense, almost agonizing pain of a heart that yearned, with every fibre of its being, for God, for ultimate union. Later, Swami would reveal that even in his dreams, he had vivid, recurring visions of Shiva, Subrahmanya, and Lord Krishna, divine manifestations that underscored his sacred destiny. This growing, all-consuming divine longing made him increasingly silent and solitary, drawing him inexorably away from the clamour and distractions of the worldly life he once knew.

Though he continued, out of duty, to help with simple family chores, like herding cattle through the green fields and assisting with farming tasks, his heart remained elsewhere, focused entirely on profound inner pursuits. Once, he told his disciples that even physical labour, when performed with complete mindfulness and a spirit of dedication, possessed the power to purify the mind, refining it like gold. Still, his yearning for absolute truth kept growing, intensifying with each passing day, becoming an irresistible current. Eventually, his family elders, noticing his deepening detachment and spiritual absorption, decided it was time for him to marry, hoping, in their traditional wisdom, that the responsibilities of married life would anchor him, would settle his restless spirit. In those days, young people had little to no say in their marriages; the elders typically chose a suitable bride, and the union was arranged according to time-honoured tradition and familial alliances. On the appointed day, the chosen bride, accompanied by her family, was brought to Nanu's house for the sacred ceremony.

But Swami was not at peace with this prescribed path. He looked at the gathering, a sea of well-meaning faces and expectant eyes, and with quiet, unwavering conviction, he spoke words that would alter the course of his life and, subsequently, the destiny of millions: "Each person is born for a unique purpose. We must diligently search for it, with all our heart and soul, and then strive tirelessly to fulfil it. Please take care of your duties—and allow me to seek mine." With those profound, resolute words, spoken with utter clarity, he left home. It was not an escape born of fear or rebellion, but the resolute beginning of a great and solitary spiritual search, a quest for ultimate liberation and truth.

From that day onward, Nanuswami became a true spiritual wanderer, a parivrajaka. He walked through countless villages and hamlets, slept in the silent sanctity of temples or under the vast, open skies, finding shelter wherever the night found him. He engaged in deep, illuminating conversations with revered saints, learned priests, insightful maulvis, and dedicated Christian missionaries, absorbing diverse spiritual perspectives like a thirsty sponge. His transformative journey stretched across the length and breadth of Kerala, Tamil Nadu, and Karnataka, enriching his understanding of various spiritual traditions and revealing the underlying unity of all faiths.

During this transformative period, he met the revered sage Chattampi Swamikal, a towering figure of wisdom in his own right. Through this pivotal encounter, Nanuswami was introduced to Thycattu Ayya, a profound master of yoga and ancient spiritual disciplines. Swami trained intensely under Ayya, learning and mastering rigorous yogic disciplines that further deepened and refined his already burgeoning spiritual practice. After completing his training, having acquired immense inner strength, profound wisdom, and an unparalleled mastery over his senses, he withdrew to the secluded, silent heights of Maruthwamala.

There, amidst the dense, whispering forests, he spent many months immersed in profound silence and unceasing meditation. The forest around him was alive with the raw, untamed presence of wild animals—bears, leopards, and others—but Swami remained utterly unafraid, embodying a serene, almost divine fearlessness. Remarkably, two majestic tigers would often sit nearby, their powerful forms resting peacefully, as if silently guarding him, becoming his most loyal and attentive companions. "They were my companions," he would later recall, speaking of the deep, intuitive connection he felt with the wild, untamed essence of nature. He lived sparingly, subsisting on only green leaves and pure spring water, and often fasted for days, purifying his body and mind, stripping away all unnecessary layers of existence. His hair and beard grew long and matted from neglect, his body grew thin and ascetic from rigorous practices—but his spirit shone with an unparalleled brightness, radiating an inner glow that seemed to defy the physical realm.

Then, in one rare and transcendent moment, amidst the deep silence of the mountain, it happened. He experienced the profound realization of Truth—a sudden, absolute spiritual awakening that illuminated his entire being, shattering all illusion and doubt. From that moment on, his path became absolutely, unequivocally clear. He was no longer searching; the quest had reached its glorious culmination. Now, his purpose was no longer for personal salvation alone, but to share his hard-won peace, his profound realizations, with others, to uplift humanity.

As he descended the hill, the word of his enlightenment spread like wildfire. People, witnessing the divine light that now emanated from him, instinctively began calling him Nanuswami, a recognition of his transformed state. They flocked to him, seeking his blessings and spiritual guidance. He spoke gently, his voice carrying the weight of universal truth, offering wisdom on both profound spiritual matters and practical worldly concerns. He even cured many illnesses using his deep, inherited knowledge of Ayurveda, a testament to his holistic understanding of life and being.

He resumed his travels, but this time, not out of personal restlessness, but with a clear, divine sense of purpose—to spread the truth he had realized, to awaken humanity. Eventually, his purposeful journey led him to a place we've heard about already—Aruvippuram, where the seminal, public events of his revolutionary mission would finally unfold.

There, people flocked to him in even greater numbers, drawn by the irresistible magnetism of his spiritual presence. Swami spoke to them with boundless compassion, treated their ailments with his healing touch, comforted the distressed, and offered solace with just a glance, his very presence a balm to suffering souls. Many became his devoted disciples, adopting the disciplined path of brahmacharya, dedicating themselves to spiritual celibacy and the earnest pursuit of truth, inspired by his example. The stream of visitors continued to grow, drawn by his profound spiritual magnetism. By now, Swami wore only plain white clothes, embodying a life of profound simplicity, detachment, and purity.

He also began to speak boldly, with quiet authority, about the urgent, undeniable need for religious reform. He fearlessly challenged harmful customs and ingrained superstitions that brutally divided society, actively encouraging people to rethink their inherited beliefs and embrace a more enlightened, compassionate path. At many places, he personally removed idols of fearsome spirits, which perpetuated fear, ignorance, and blind adherence, and replaced them with symbols of pure, peaceful worship, fostering a sense of harmony and true devotion. He even, in acts of quiet rebellion, tossed certain ancient idols into rivers and systematically dismantled superstitious shrines, literally clearing the way for genuine spiritual understanding and direct experience of the divine. In their place, he set up new temples that encouraged noble thinking, fostered true community, and championed the radical idea of universal brotherhood, open to all.

That is how, guided by his profound realization and divine purpose, he made the momentous decision to establish a temple at Aruvippuram and consecrate the idol with his own hands. That historic moment—already described in Chapter 1—was not an isolated, impulsive event, but the profound fruit of this long and noble quest, the culmination of his arduous spiritual journey, and the thunderous beginning of a sweeping social revolution that would reverberate through history.

The message Swami gave that day was a direct reflection of the truth he had realized, a crystal-clear vision for a transformed humanity: "A model place where all people live like brothers, without distinctions of caste or hatred of religion." This was not just about Aruvippuram, a single village on a riverbank. It was not even just about Kerala, his home state. Swami's dream, born of his profound spiritual awakening, was for the entire world, a global vision of unity, harmony, and inherent human dignity.

But the world, at that time, was deeply caught in the suffocating grip of ignorance, blind superstition, and deeply seated division. His life's ultimate, overarching mission became abundantly clear: to free the world from these destructive, man-made chains and fill it, irrevocably, with light, with boundless love, and with the unifying spirit of true brotherhood.

6

Humanity Is One Family

Great souls across the world, throughout history, have dedicated their entire lives to one singularly noble goal: to establish true human brotherhood and transform the world into a more beautiful, harmonious, and equitable place for all beings. The extraordinary life of Sreenarayana Guru was no different; in fact, it stood as a towering example of this universal pursuit. His entire existence was a sacred offering, a profound yajna—a selfless sacrifice performed ceaselessly, every waking moment, in the unwavering service of humankind. Until he attained samadhi at the venerable age of seventy-two, his days were filled with tireless, purposeful action and profound spiritual devotion, all meticulously aimed at uplifting every individual he encountered, irrespective of their station or birth.

Wherever Guru went, an almost tangible light seemed to follow in his wake. People gathered around him like moths irresistibly drawn to a gentle, unwavering flame, pulled by an invisible spiritual force that emanated from his very being. Many of them had once been tragically lost in the labyrinth of blind rituals, meaningless customs, and destructive religious divisions, their lives circumscribed by rigid societal norms that crushed their spirit. But when they came near the Guru, their hearts, hardened by years of oppression and despair, began to subtly change, softened by the sheer presence of his unconditional love and boundless compassion. He didn't preach with loud, booming words or dramatic, thunderous pronouncements. Instead, his profound, often illuminating silence, his calm, all-knowing gaze that seemed to pierce to the very soul, and his inherently kind and benevolent presence were more than enough to inspire deep inner transformation within those fortunate enough to seek him out.

Some people who, due to the cruelly oppressive caste rules of the era, had never been permitted to even step foot inside a temple before, found newfound courage in his presence to pray, to connect with the divine in their own way. Some who had given up all hope in life, their spirits burdened by relentless injustice and gnawing despair, began, miraculously, to find reasons to rebuild their shattered lives with renewed purpose and quiet dignity. Some who had lived only for themselves, caught in the suffocating grip of selfishness and narrow-mindedness, began, perhaps for the first time, to live for others, discovering the profound, liberating joy of selfless service and universal love. They were not just hearing abstract words of wisdom or dry philosophical concepts; they were experiencing the Guru's boundless, unconditional love, the profound, unshakeable peace of his presence, and the gentle, unwavering guidance that transformed their very perception of themselves and the world around them.

The Guru taught many profound truths—about the nature of God, the intricate essence of the soul, the meaning and purpose of human life, and the vast, awe-inspiring expanse of the universe itself. But amidst all his teachings, one message shone the brightest, radiating like an eternal beacon of hope, piercing through the darkness of prejudice: "Humanity is one family." In a society deeply, tragically torn by arbitrary distinctions of caste, religion, and class, a society that meticulously built walls between its people, Guru gave this simple yet profoundly revolutionary idea: All human beings are inherently equal, bound by a common, undeniable humanity. He posed a powerful, yet simple, question that challenged centuries of ingrained prejudice and dogma: "People say God created the world. So, shouldn't all beings—whether rich or poor, Brahmin or Ezhava, upper caste or lower caste—be children of the same Creator? Shouldn't we, by this divine decree, see each other as brothers and sisters, connected by a shared spiritual lineage, by the very essence of creation?"

Guru didn't just articulate this truth with eloquent words; he embodied it, he lived it every single moment of his life, becoming a walking testament to his own philosophy. He invited everyone, without exception, to his ashram, regardless of their caste or religious background, effectively dissolving the invisible yet formidable walls that society had painstakingly built to separate and oppress. He extended equal love, compassion, and tireless effort to all—whether they were revered scholars steeped in ancient texts or humble labourers toiling in the fields. He treated every individual with the same unwavering dignity and profound respect, seeing the divine spark in each. He taught his disciples to see and respect every human being as a direct reflection of the divine, an embodiment of the sacred. He firmly believed that the soul has no caste; it is beyond such artificial, man-made classifications. The body might bear a name or carry the weight of a societal background, but the soul, he asserted, is pure, eternally free, and absolutely equal in all beings. Once, when someone, perhaps seeking to provoke or simply unable to grasp his radical stance, asked him about caste, he replied with characteristic wisdom, cutting straight to the heart of the matter: "Ask not about caste. Ask if he has character." This concise yet profound statement instantly redirected focus from superficial birth distinctions to the true, moral measure of a human being. Another time, a foreigner who had the distinct privilege of meeting the Guru described him aptly as "the prophet of universal brotherhood." That is exactly who he was—a living, breathing embodiment of unity, compassion, and inclusive love.

Guru also knew, with profound insight, that merely preaching equality wasn't enough for true, lasting societal transformation. People needed to be actively freed from the chains of ignorance that perpetuated their suffering and subjugation, that kept them mentally enslaved. He consistently emphasized two powerful, actionable principles: "Gain strength through organization. Gain freedom through education." He actively and tirelessly encouraged the setting up of schools, libraries, and reading rooms throughout society, recognizing knowledge as the ultimate liberator. He passionately wanted people—especially those from marginalized communities who had been systematically denied access to knowledge for centuries—to learn, to read, and most importantly, to think for themselves, to question injustice, to seek truth with an open mind, and to forge their own paths to enlightenment.

But his vision of education wasn't just about letters and numbers or accumulating academic degrees. It was about cultivating wisdom—the profound wisdom to see all humans as one interconnected family, to reject hatred and prejudice in all its insidious forms, and to wholeheartedly embrace love, mutual respect, and universal compassion.

Guru's teachings deeply touched hearts across Kerala and began to spread far beyond its geographical borders, carried by the winds of change. Slowly, almost imperceptibly at first, then with an increasing, undeniable momentum, change began to take root in the very fabric of society. Temples, once exclusive domains guarded by rigid caste laws, cautiously, then confidently, opened their doors to all, welcoming every devotee regardless of birth. Schools, once segregated bastions of privilege, welcomed children from every caste, breaking down deeply ingrained educational barriers. People began, hesitantly at first, then with growing confidence, to question age-old customs and superstitions that had long held society captive in fear and ignorance. And above all, they began to see one another with genuine respect, recognizing the shared humanity that transcended all superficial differences.

Guru once succinctly stated, with the clarity of a mountain spring: "Whatever be the religion, it is enough if it makes you a better human being." This profound, simple statement encapsulates the very essence of all his teachings, cutting through theological complexity to the core of human virtue. Whether one followed Hinduism, Islam, Christianity, or any other faith—what truly mattered, what truly elevated a soul, was the cultivation of goodness, compassion, and truthfulness in one's life. His ultimate dream was not of a world with one monolithic religion, forcing all into a single mould, but a world with many diverse spiritual paths leading to the same universal truth—a world where people of all castes and creeds could walk together in harmony, celebrating their unique differences while profoundly recognizing their fundamental unity and shared spiritual essence.

To tirelessly spread this transformative message, Guru travelled ceaselessly—sometimes on foot, walking the dusty paths with his disciples; sometimes by palanquin, a symbol of humble conveyance; or by boat, navigating the tranquil back-waters, reaching remote villages and bustling towns alike. Wherever he went, he brought people together, fostering community, understanding, and a shared sense of purpose. And wherever he went, he left behind the subtle, enduring fragrance of peace, the unshakeable strength of unity, and the illuminating light of love, transforming countless individual lives and profoundly shaping the destiny of a nation.

7

Light Spreads

We have already seen how Sreenarayana Guru worked tirelessly to remove the crushing weight of superstitions and the insidious grip of harmful practices that plagued society. In this chapter, we will delve deeper into those profound and far-reaching efforts, witnessing firsthand how his transformative vision began to reshape and uplift entire communities across Kerala.

Not far from Aruvippuram, nestled amidst verdant surroundings, stood a humble house named Vadavinkode Bhavanam. During his early days, Guru often chose to stay here, transforming this modest dwelling into an unexpected magnet for seekers. Devotees, curious minds, and common people from all walks of life—from the lowliest labourer to the occasional inquisitive scholar—came ceaselessly to listen to Guru's serene words and receive his gentle blessings. Vadavinkode Bhavanam, originally a simple family home, gradually, organically evolved into a kind of informal ashram—a vibrant, living place where spiritual ideas blossomed like rare flowers, where profound wisdom was shared freely, and where the vital seeds of social reform were quietly, yet powerfully, sown into fertile ground.

But Guru's expansive vision was never limited to just temples and prayers, important and transformative as they were. He profoundly, deeply wanted to change society itself, to uplift it from its deeply entrenched inequalities, its suffocating ignorance, and its systemic injustices. He knew, with absolute clarity, that real, lasting change—the kind that truly liberates—would only happen if people could learn to think clearly, cultivate a profound sense of self-respect, and act with collective courage and purpose. For that to happen, they crucially needed access to education, a strong, unshakeable sense of their own inherent worth as human beings, and above all, the unifying power of collective action and unity.

To effectively spread these transformative ideas beyond individual interactions, Guru actively encouraged the formation of associations and organizations. He held a deep, unshakeable conviction that collective effort, when harnessed purposefully and directed by a shared vision, was infinitely more powerful and impactful than isolated individual action. This fundamental belief is precisely why he famously uttered the potent maxim: "Gain strength through organization." At his direct guidance and profound inspiration, many dynamic and influential groups formed across the length and breadth of Kerala—most notably, the Sree Narayana Dharma Paripalana Yogam (SNDP Yogam). These dynamic, community-led groups worked tirelessly, with unwavering dedication, to uplift the poor and the marginalized, to vehemently fight against pervasive caste discrimination, and to vigorously promote education as the indispensable means of liberation and empowerment for all.

Guru possessed an extraordinary, intuitive understanding of community needs that transcended conventional thinking, and he taught that every village needed far more than just a place of worship. Once, while standing near a newly established temple, he articulated a vision that boldly transcended mere ritualistic devotion, extending into the very fabric of community life: "All around this temple, let there be thriving gardens, green and beautiful. Plant shade trees with inviting platforms around them so people can rest, converse, and find solace. Build clean, accessible reading rooms in every temple compound, and let them contain all religious texts, from every faith, for people to study. Let the temple itself remain in one corner, serving its sacred purpose, but let the wider space serve the community." This message was incredibly powerful and profoundly forward-thinking, a blueprint for integrated spiritual and social hubs. It profoundly illustrates that Guru wanted temples to become true centres of learning, vibrant communal gathering places, serene havens for rest, and profound spaces of peace—not merely exclusive places for rigid rituals or the guarded domain of a privileged few. He firmly believed that people must learn to live in harmony with one another, think for themselves critically, and develop a deep, respectful understanding of all religions and spiritual paths, recognizing their shared core.

To achieve this ambitious spiritual and social transformation, Guru undertook the momentous task of consecrating over forty temples across Kerala and in neighbouring regions during his lifetime. But these were not ordinary temples, conforming to traditional, rigid norms. In many of them, there were no traditional idols, no anthropomorphic representations of deities—instead, he often consecrated powerful symbols like plain mirrors, or glowing lamps. Why did he choose such unconventional, almost radical, symbols? Because Guru wanted people to profoundly understand that God is within you, not an external entity confined to a fixed idol or a specific place. When you look into a mirror, you are compelled to see your own reflection, powerfully symbolizing the divine spark inherent within every individual. When you light a lamp, you are not just illuminating a physical space but metaphorically awakening inner wisdom and spiritual awareness within your own being. One famous temple Guru established, for instance, had only a mirror as its focal point, reflecting anyone who stood before it. This was a clear, unambiguous, and profoundly liberating message: "Look within. The divine is not somewhere else, external and unreachable. It is you. It resides within you."

He also adamantly insisted that people themselves, the community members, should manage these temples—not just priests or members of the so-called higher castes who traditionally controlled them. He strongly encouraged democratic management and active participation by the entire community, fostering a vital sense of ownership, shared responsibility, and inherent equality. His teachings profoundly gave people self-worth, instilling in them the courage to challenge oppressive norms and to take charge of their own spiritual and social destiny, empowering them to become agents of their own change.

At the same time, he continued his relentless, compassionate fight against dangerous beliefs and superstitions that instilled fear, perpetuated ignorance, and hindered genuine human progress. If he found shrines or practices that encouraged fear, blind adherence, or superstitious rituals, he would unequivocally remove them, often personally, paving the way for rational thought, scientific inquiry, and true, pure devotion. He once famously said, his words cutting through centuries of blind faith, “What is the use of worship if it doesn’t make you a better human being?”—emphasizing the paramount ethical and moral dimension of spirituality over mere ritualism.

His simple, yet profoundly resonant words became guiding lights for the people, illuminating their path forward out of darkness and into understanding. Some of his most memorable and transformative maxims, etched into the collective consciousness, included:

- "Whatever be the religion, it is enough if it makes you good."
- "Ask not about caste. Ask if he has character."
- "Acts that create division are not dharma."
- "Without cleanliness, there is no worship."

His light began to spread—from village to village, town to town, gently but powerfully, like the dawn breaking over the land. People began to clean their surroundings, understanding the profound link between outer cleanliness and inner purity. They built schools, recognizing education as the indispensable key to upliftment and progress. They started libraries, fostering a love for knowledge, critical thinking, and intellectual growth. And they began to come together to celebrate festivals that consciously included everyone, actively breaking down social barriers and fostering deep communal harmony and joyous participation. Women, who were often neglected, marginalized, and subjected to severe restrictions in traditional society, also found new strength, agency, and empowerment through Guru's liberating teachings, which championed their inherent equality and dignity.

Sreenarayana Guru was no ordinary social reformer, content with superficial changes. He didn't use anger or force to bring about change, nor did he criticize others loudly or publicly condemn individuals with harsh words. Like the sun, he simply shined—and his inherent warmth, his radiant presence, and the undeniable, inherent truth of his message awakened the hearts and minds of thousands, inspiring them to rise above their conditioned prejudices. His core message was a powerful confluence of boundless love, unwavering unity, fundamental truth, and profound inner awakening. And slowly, but surely, that brilliant, transformative light began to cover all of Kerala, forever changing its social, cultural, and spiritual landscape, paving the way for a more just and enlightened future.

8

Strength Through Organization

Earlier, we briefly mentioned the Sree Narayana Dharma Paripalana Yogam, often simply referred to as SNDP Yogam, as an organization fostered by Guru's transformative vision. Now, let's delve deeper into its pivotal origins, its far-reaching purpose, and its profound, enduring impact on society, especially for those who had been historically marginalized.

The SNDP Yogam was officially founded in 1903, a landmark year that marked a new era of organized social reform in Kerala. Its inspiration came directly and unequivocally from the enlightened vision of Sreenarayana Guru himself. One of the key individuals who worked tirelessly, dedicating his life to establish this groundbreaking organization, was Dr. Palpu. He was a devoted follower of the Guru, a man of exceptional intellect and unwavering commitment, and a distinguished medical doctor by profession. Dr. Palpu, recognizing the urgent need for a structured approach to social change, played a crucial, indispensable role in giving organizational shape and practical direction to Guru's revolutionary ideas, translating abstract philosophy into concrete action.

Guru always held an unwavering, deep-seated belief that real, lasting strength lies inherently in unity. He had personally witnessed, with a compassionate yet clear eye, how deeply society was divided—fragmented not just by rigid caste hierarchies, but also by stark economic class disparities, and the pervasive, suffocating darkness of ignorance and superstition. He also keenly observed how these profound divisions rendered people weak, fearful, and utterly helpless, perpetuating their suffering across generations. To fundamentally change this oppressive reality, to break these invisible chains, Guru understood that people had to come together, transcending their artificial differences, bridging the divides that society had meticulously constructed. That is precisely why Guru taught with such conviction, his words echoing through time: "Gain strength through organization."

The SNDP Yogam was thus formed with the explicit, unambiguous purpose of spreading Guru's liberating message and tirelessly working to uplift the downtrodden masses, to bring them light and dignity. It was not merely a religious group confined to spiritual rites or exclusive prayer; it was a dynamic, multifaceted, and comprehensive social movement that aimed for holistic societal transformation. It tirelessly worked for universal education, advocating fiercely for equal access to knowledge for all, irrespective of birth; for profound equality, bravely challenging the deep-seated prejudices of caste and untouchability; for true self-respect, instilling dignity and inner worth in those who had been systematically demeaned and stripped of their humanity; and for practical economic development, empowering individuals to improve their material conditions and secure a brighter future.

While Guru didn't directly involve himself in the day-to-day managerial affairs of the Yogam, his influence was omnipresent. He guided it with his unparalleled wisdom and profound spiritual insight, like a steady hand on a rudder. He inspired its overarching vision, its moral compass, and provided clear, concise instructions about its profound purpose and direction. Dr. Palpu and other dedicated, brilliant leaders, deeply influenced and energized by his teachings, followed his direction faithfully, translating his philosophical ideals into practical, actionable steps that resonated deeply with the common people.

At that historical juncture, most people from so-called backward castes faced severe, systemic discrimination; they didn't have access to basic schools, were brazenly barred from entering temples, and were denied dignified government jobs, trapping them in cycles of poverty. They lived in abject poverty and were often cruelly treated as untouchables, subjected to daily indignities that stripped them of their human rights. The SNDP Yogam bravely confronted these deeply entrenched injustices head-on, with quiet courage and unwavering resolve. It began to actively build schools, recognizing education as the primary, most potent tool for liberation; it started libraries, fostering a vital culture of reading and intellectual growth; and it vigorously encouraged widespread temple reform, pushing relentlessly for inclusivity and open access for all, dismantling sacred barriers. The Yogam supported people to study, learn valuable trades, and ultimately lead lives of dignity, self-reliance, and economic self-sufficiency, breaking free from generations of oppression and servitude.

Guru wisely advised the Yogam to appoint good public speakers—individuals capable of clearly articulating his spiritual and practical teachings with conviction and clarity—to travel tirelessly across villages and towns. These speakers were given a clear, vital mandate: to speak on topics that were crucial for societal upliftment, addressing the core needs of the people. These included:

- Religion, interpreted not asrigiddogma, but in its most universal, inclusive, and unifying sense.
- Morality, emphasizing ethical conduct, selfless compassion, and virtuous living as the foundation of society.
- Education, seen as a fundamental pathway to enlightenment, empowerment, and breaking the chains of ignorance.
- Industry, promoting economic self-reliance, vocational skills, and progressive development to improve material well-being.

Guru gave special, profound attention to the concept of religion, redefining its true essence for a fractured society. He taught: "Religion should help people become better human beings. It should teach love, truth, and unity. Any religious practice that creates hatred, division, or fear is not true religion." These were incredibly bold, even revolutionary ideas for their time, directly challenging the prevailing interpretations of faith that had been twisted and used to justify oppression and discrimination. But the people, weary of suffering, were ready to listen—because they instinctively trusted Guru's inherent wisdom, and because they were desperately tired of suffering under the yoke of unjust traditions and cruel, arbitrary divisions.

The SNDP Yogam also worked assiduously to identify and train leaders from within the marginalized communities themselves. Guru firmly believed that every single person possessed hidden strength and immense, untapped potential. If guided well, he taught, they could emerge as powerful, compassionate leaders, capable of guiding others towards a better, more equitable future. He ardently wanted the organization to bring out the inner light in every person, fostering self-reliance, dignity, and collective leadership within the very communities that had been denied such opportunities.

One of the most gifted and celebrated disciples of Guru was Kumaran Asan, a young man of exceptional poetic talent who would later become a towering figure in Malayalam literature and a renowned poet of profound social conscience. Guru, recognizing his immense potential and unique literary gift, personally took it upon himself to send him to study further in prominent centres of learning like Bangalore and Calcutta, ensuring he received the best possible education. When Asan left for his advanced studies, Guru, known for his serene composure, wept like a child—a poignant moment that powerfully revealed how deeply he cared for his disciples, not just for their spiritual enlightenment, but for their intellectual and personal growth. Asan subsequently returned, transformed into a powerful poet and profound social thinker, emerging as one of the leading voices of social change in Kerala. His poems, infused with the luminous essence of Guru's teachings, gave people immense courage and unwavering hope, inspiring them to rise against injustice and envision a better world.

In later years, many other dedicated individuals also joined the burgeoning movement: passionate reformers, eloquent writers, committed teachers, and industrious workers from various walks of life. They collectively opened numerous schools, built reading rooms, and actively promoted radical concepts like inter-caste dining and temple entry for all, directly dismantling the physical and symbolic barriers of caste. Through the tireless and dedicated efforts of the SNDP Yogam, Guru's transformative teachings and his vision for a harmonious society spread far and wide—not just across the length and breadth of Kerala, but to parts of Tamil Nadu, Karnataka, and even across the seas to Sri Lanka, impacting the diaspora. The Yogam thus became a potent symbol of awakening, empowerment, and organized social reform for the oppressed and marginalized communities throughout the entire region.

Guru had once wisely said, encapsulating his philosophy in a single, powerful metaphor: "We must become lamps—lighting ourselves and others. We must become strong through unity, and free through knowledge." The SNDP Yogam, under his divine inspiration and unwavering guidance, helped thousands of people light their inner lamps, dispelling the suffocating darkness of ignorance and prejudice that had veiled their lives. That light, once kindled, still burns brightly today, a testament to the enduring legacy of Sreenarayana Guru and his timeless vision of a unified, enlightened humanity.

9

Beams of Dharma

It is truly difficult, perhaps impossible, to find another life so pure, so utterly blameless, and so thoroughly dedicated to universal good as that of Sreenarayana Guru. In his long, prolific public life, spanning over forty unwavering years, not a single blemish or trace of selfishness was ever found. He possessed no private life in the ordinary sense, for his entire being was an open book, transparent and radiantly clear, filled solely with boundless compassion, profound wisdom, and tireless, selfless service to humanity.

Many stories, some bordering on the miraculous, are still told with awe and reverence about Guru's extraordinary, almost supernatural powers. People whispered and believed, with unwavering faith, that he could make the mute speak, heal chronic, debilitating diseases that doctors had deemed incurable, disappear from one place and instantly appear in another, and even read the innermost thoughts and purest intentions of others with his divine, penetrating vision. These awe-inspiring accounts, passed down through generations, became widely popular among the common people and are still shared today with immense reverence, centuries later, testifying to the extraordinary aura that surrounded him.

But Guru himself never encouraged such talk or sensationalism. He never claimed to be a miracle-worker or allowed anyone to treat him like a magician or a purveyor of cheap wonders. His true power was not in performing dazzling feats or displaying supernatural abilities; rather, it lay, profoundly, in his unparalleled ability to change minds, to heal wounded hearts, and to bring genuine, lasting peace and clarity to troubled, confused souls. Once, when someone, perhaps seeking a secret or a sign, directly asked him about these supposed miracles, he simply smiled, his eyes twinkling with a deeper truth, and said: "If a person lives a pure life, with unwavering self-control and absolute devotion to truth, even nature will assist him, aligning itself with his purpose." This was his profound secret—a life lived in complete, seamless alignment with universal principles, a life that became a living embodiment of Dharma. His entire existence was built upon this unshakeable foundation of Dharma—righteous living. He saw Dharma not as a rigid set of strict rules or dogmatic commandments, but as a dynamic, expansive, and liberating path of truth, boundless love, and selfless service. He often emphasized, encapsulating his philosophy: "The greatest Dharma is to remove the suffering of others." That was precisely why he consistently stood with the poor, the sick, the unclean, and the socially rejected, extending his hand, offering them solace, restoring their dignity, and providing practical, tangible help. He believed, with unwavering conviction, that serving people, particularly those most in need, was the highest and most authentic form of worship, a direct offering to the divine.

In his later years, Guru chose to establish his main ashram at Sivagiri, a quiet and extraordinarily beautiful place nestled gently near Varkala, overlooking the majestic expanse of the Arabian Sea. Sivagiri swiftly became his primary centre of activity, a vibrant spiritual hub where his teachings flourished like a verdant garden and where his profound vision took concrete, organizational shape. Dedicated disciples came from far and wide to live there, committing their lives wholeheartedly to his ideals. Visitors from across India—including renowned poets, influential politicians, courageous social reformers, and earnest spiritual seekers from all walks of life—came to meet him, drawn by his profound wisdom, his serene presence, and the unmistakable spiritual energy that permeated the ashram.

One of the most important and innovative contributions Guru made during this period was in meticulously shaping the Sivagiri pilgrimage. Unlike other traditional pilgrimages where people journeyed to distant temples or sacred rivers for purely ritualistic purposes, often for personal merit, Guru's pilgrimage had a unique, deeply transformative purpose, focusing on collective enlightenment and social upliftment. When someone, seeking clarification, asked him what should be the true aim and meaning of the Sivagiri pilgrimage, he explained it in two comprehensive, interconnected parts, focusing on both individual purity and societal development:

For individual life, the pilgrimage's focus should be on cultivating the Five Purities (Pancha Suddhi), a holistic approach to self refinement:

Physical purity: Emphasizing cleanliness of the body and surroundings, recognizing the body as a temple.

Food purity: Advocating for healthy, nourishing, and sattvic (pure) food habits, promoting well-being.

Mental purity: Cultivating positive, constructive thoughts, fostering kindness, empathy, and freedom from malice, jealousy, or hatred.

Speech purity: Encouraging truthful, compassionate, and constructive communication, devoid of harshness or gossip.

Action purity: Promoting righteous, ethical, and selfless conduct in all endeavours, aligning actions with universal Dharma.

For social life, the pilgrimage should actively promote learning and awareness in practical areas crucial for sustainable community development and progress:

Education: Advocating for universal access to knowledge for all, irrespective of caste or creed.

Cleanliness: Emphasizing personal hygiene and public health, recognizing its link to spiritual well-being.

Devotion to God: Fostering genuine spiritual understanding and direct experience of the divine, beyond mere external ritual.

Organization: Encouraging collective action, unity, and the formation of strong, supportive community groups.

Agriculture:Promoting sustainable farming practices for food security and economic stability.

Trade: Encouraging ethical commerce, fair practices, and responsible entrepreneurship.

Handicrafts: Supporting traditional skills, artisan work, and vocational training for livelihood improvement.

Technical training: Promoting modern vocational skills and practical knowledge for enhanced economic opportunities.

These were intensely practical, forward-thinking goals, designed to uplift both the individual and society in a truly holistic and sustainable manner. Guru firmly believed that a pilgrimage should not merely be about fleeting rituals or seeking blessings for personal gain, but fundamentally about continuous learning, profound personal transformation, and contributing actively to the well-being and upliftment of the collective.

During this period, he also composed many profound verses and poems. Though small in number, his literary works are incredibly concise yet brimming with deep spiritual meaning, reflecting his direct experience of truth, not just mere book knowledge or abstract philosophy. One of his most famous and unifying verses, a beacon of universalism, reads: "The essence of all religions is the same. The paths may differ, but the goal is one." Another powerful and oft-quoted saying of his, a concise yet revolutionary statement, was: "One caste, one religion, one God for mankind." This statement does not imply that all religions must be merged into one single, monolithic faith, or that everyone must abandon their inherited beliefs. Rather, Guru meant that beneath all superficial differences, all diverse expressions of belief and culture, we are all inherently part of one human family, connected by a shared spiritual essence. He urged humanity to learn to live in peace, harmony, and mutual respect, recognizing the underlying unity of existence that transcends all perceived divisions.

He was also a keen observer of science and modern progress, embracing the advancements of his time. He welcomed new inventions and encouraged people to adopt useful technologies that could genuinely improve lives and alleviate suffering. He believed in a harmonious, dynamic balance between timeless spiritual values and the vital advancements of scientific development, advocating for a holistic approach to life that integrated both inner wisdom and outer progress.

One of the most touching and enduring aspects of his character was his profound, innate humility. Even when thousands bowed before him, revering him as a divine figure, a living saint, he remained utterly simple and quiet, completely unaffected by external adulation or fame. He lived in a small, unadorned room, wore only plain white clothes, and ate humble, simple food, embodying the ideal of detachment, inner contentment, and spiritual purity. His final years were spent in serene calmness, continuously radiating peace, guiding others with his compassionate gaze, his profound silence, and his boundless wisdom to all who came near, a living testament to his own teachings.

Even after his physical body passed away and he attained samadhi, the powerful beams of Dharma he spread continue to shine brightly—through the countless schools he inspired, the inclusive temples he consecrated, the ashrams that carry on his sacred legacy, the libraries that disseminate knowledge, and, most importantly, in the transformed hearts and minds of millions of people whose lives he touched and forever changed. His life was a radiant, inextinguishable light, and that light still burns brightly today, illuminating the path towards a more unified, compassionate, and enlightened world for all.

10

Sacred Relics and Pilgrimage Gurudevagiri, Navi Mumbai

Among the few preserved physical remnants associated with Sree Narayana Guru, a deeply revered collection is housed at the Gurudevagiri complex of the Sree Narayana Mandira Samiti (SNMS) in Nerul West, Navi Mumbai. These sacred dental relics—comprising an original tooth and three artificial teeth—are preserved with utmost sanctity in a specially constructed shrine within the temple complex.

The Gurudevagiri complex is a spiritual and cultural hub that houses two important temples:

A temple dedicated to Sree Narayana Guru, where his idol is enshrined and worshipped.

A Siva temple, consecrated in the tradition of Guru's message and spiritual practice.

Each year, in the first week of February, the Gurudevagiri Theerthadanam (Pilgrimage Festival) is held to commemorate two momentous events:

1. The consecration of the Sivalinga in the Siva temple.
2. The installation of the Guru's idol in the adjacent temple dedicated to guru

During this annual festival, the sacred relics of the Guru are ceremoniously brought out for devotees to have darsan (holy viewing), offering a powerful moment of connection and reflection for followers.

How to Reach Gurudevagiri, Navi Mumbai.

Location:

Gurudevagiri, Sree Narayana Mandira Samiti Complex
Sector 6, Nerul West, Navi Mumbai, Maharashtra – 400 706.

Nearest Airports:
Chhatrapati Shivaji Maharaj International Airport
(Sahar Terminal), Mumbai
(Approximately 35 km from Nerul.

Navimubai Airport:

(To be operational in September 2025. Approx. 10 km from Nerul.

Nearest Railway Stations:

Depending on your direction of travel, several options are available:

Panvel Station – approx. 20 km

Kurla Station – approx. 22 km

Bandra Terminus – approx. 26 km

Local Transport:

Suburban local trains (Harbour Line) to Nerul Station

BEST and NMMT buses from various parts of Mumbai

Auto-rickshaws and app-based taxis (Ola, Uber) are readily availlable.

The sacred relics of Sreenarayana Guru - an original tooth and three artificial teeth.

Gurudevagiri Complex Nerul

Shrine housing the relics of
Sreenarayana Guru

11

Afterword

The life and teachings of Sreenarayana Guru represent not just a pivotal chapter in the history of Kerala, but a timeless testament to the extraordinary power of spiritual realization coupled with compassionate social action. From the quiet villages of Chempazhanthi and Aruvippuram, his influence radiated outwards, fundamentally altering the spiritual, social, and cultural landscape of a region, and inspiring movements for equality across India and far beyond its borders.

Guru's mission was never about creating a new religion, but about purifying existing ones and revealing the universal truths that bind all faiths. His resonant call for "One caste, one religion, one God for mankind" was not a demand for rigid uniformity, but an eloquent, profound plea for humanity to recognize its shared essence and transcend divisive barriers. He taught that true worship was not confined to temples or ritualistic acts, but expressed through ethical living, intellectual growth, and selfless service to fellow beings.

The establishment of institutions like the SNDP Yogam and the unique, forward-thinking vision behind the Sivagiri pilgrimage exemplify his pragmatic approach to social reform. He understood that spiritual awakening must translate into tangible improvements in the lives of the marginalized—through accessible education, economic empowerment, and robust communal organization. His unwavering emphasis on self-reliance, impeccable moral conduct, and a scientific outlook ensured that his revolution was deeply rooted, sustainable, and capable of enduring through generations.

Even after his samadhi, the powerful light of Sreenarayana Guru continues to shine brightly. His philosophy, rooted in Advaita Vedanta yet intensely practical in its application, remains profoundly relevant in a world still grappling with division, intolerance, and inequality. The schools he inspired, the inclusive temples he established, and the organizations he founded stand as living memorials to his expansive vision. More importantly, the seeds of unity, compassion, and the relentless pursuit of knowledge he sowed continue to blossom in the hearts of countless individuals who strive for a more harmonious and just world. His life serves as an eternal reminder that the greatest strength lies in organization, the deepest freedom in knowledge, and the truest divinity in universal love.

12

Timeline of Sree Narayana Guru's Life and Mission

Here's a chronological overview of key events based on the chapters:

1856 CE (Chingam, 1032 ME): Narayanan (Nanu) is born in **Vayalvarathu Veedu,** Chempazhanthi, approximately 24 km north of Thiruvananthapuram, into the Ezhava community.

1861 CE (approx.): **Nanu** undergoes **Vidyarambham**, his formal initiation into learning, at age five.

Teenage Years (approx. 1870s): **Nanu** masters **Malayalam** and Sanskrit, with his uncle **Krishnan Vaidyar** seeking his interpretations of difficult Sanskrit verses. He also begins learning **Tamil**.

Late 1870s - Early 1880s: Nanu lives as a wandering spiritual seeker (parivrajaka), travelling across Kerala, Tamil Nadu, and Karnataka. He encounters and studies under **Thycattu Ayya**, mastering yogic disciplines. He also experiences a period of illness (smallpox) at a temple.

Mid-1880s (approx.): Nanu withdraws to **Maruthwamala** for intense meditation and ascetic practices, eventually experiencing profound spiritual enlightenment and the realization of Truth. He becomes known as **Nanu Swami.**

February 1888 CE (Kumbham, 1063 ME): **Nanu Swami**, now 32, performs the historic consecration of the **Shivalinga** at **Aruvippuram**, challenging caste barriers with the message: "A model place where all people live like brothers, without distinctions of caste or hatred of religion." This marks the beginning of his public mission.

Late 1880s-early 1900s: Guru frequently stays at **Vadavinkode Bhavanam,** which becomes an informal ashram. He continues to dismantle superstitions, replace fearful idols with symbols of universal worship (mirrors, lamps), and emphasize the importance of unity, education, and self-respect.

1903 CE: The Sree Narayana Dharma Paripalana Yogam (SNDP Yogam) is officially founded, inspired by Guru's vision, with **Dr. Palpu** playing a crucial organizational role. The Yogam works for education, equality, self-respect, and economic development for the marginalized.

Early 1900s onwards: Guru establishes his main ashram at Sivagiri, near **Varkala**.

Throughout his mission: Guru consecrates over forty temples across Kerala and neighbouring regions, each embodying his inclusive vision. He promotes education, cleanliness, ethical conduct, and communal organization. He composes profound verses like "One caste, one religion, one God for mankind."

Later Years: Guru outlines the transformative goals of the **Sivagiri pilgrimage,** emphasizing **Pancha Suddhi** (Five Purities) and practical societal development through knowledge, industry, and community. He continues to guide the SNDP Yogam and his disciples, including **Kumaran Asan**.

1928 CE: Sree Narayana Guru attains samadhi at the age of seventy-two at Sivagiri, leaving behind an enduring legacy of social reform, spiritual enlightenment, and universal brotherhood.

13

Glossary

Here's a comprehensive glossary based on the bolded terms from the chapters:

Advaita Vedanta: A major school of Hindu philosophy, primarily based on the Upanishads, which emphasizes the oneness of the individual soul (Atman) with the ultimate reality (Brahman). Sree Narayana Guru's philosophy was deeply rooted in Advaita.

Ashram: A hermitage, monastery, or a place of spiritual retreat, often where a guru lives and teaches.

Aruvippuram: A village in Kerala where Sree Narayana Guru performed the historic consecration of a Shivalinga in 1888 CE, defying caste-based temple entry restrictions.

Ayitham / Theendal: Abhorrent practices of untouchability prevalent in Kerala society during Sree Narayana Guru's time, where contact or even the shadow of a 'lower caste' person was believed to cause 'pollution' to upper castes.

Ayurvedic physician (Vaidyan): A practitioner of Ayurveda, a traditional Indian system of medicine.

Bangalore: A city in Karnataka, a prominent center of learning, where Kumaran Asan was sent by Guru for further studies.

Brahmin: The highest priestly caste in the traditional Hindu caste system.

Brahmacharya: A spiritual discipline characterized by celibacy, purity of conduct, and dedicated pursuit of knowledge, often undertaken by spiritual aspirants.

Calcutta: A major city in India (now Kolkata), another prominent center of learning where Kumaran Asan studied.

Caste hierarchies: A rigid social stratification system in India that historically determined a person's status, occupation, and social interactions based on birth.

Chalai market street: A bustling and historic market area in Thiruvananthapuram, Kerala.

Chattayam star: A specific birth star (nakshatra) in the Malayalam calendar system, under which Sree Narayana Guru was born.

Chattampi Swamikal: A contemporary and close associate of Sree Narayana Guru, an influential Hindu sage and social reformer in Kerala.

Chempazhanthi: The serene village in Kerala where Sree Narayana Guru was born.

Chingam: A Malayalam month, corresponding to August-September, when Sree Narayana Guru was born.

Dharma: A fundamental concept in Indian religions, referring to righteous conduct, moral duty, cosmic law, and the path of truth. Guru redefined it as removing the suffering of others.

Dr. Palpu: A distinguished medical doctor and a devoted disciple of Sree Narayana Guru, who played a crucial role in the establishment of the SNDP Yogam.

Education: For Guru, education was not just about literacy but about cultivating wisdom, self-respect, and critical thinking to achieve liberation and upliftment.

Epics: Refers to ancient Indian epic poems like the Ramayana and Mahabharata, which are rich in philosophical and moral narratives.

Ezhava community: A prominent community in Kerala that faced severe social discrimination and marginalization under the traditional caste system. Sree Narayana Guru was born into this community.

Guru: A spiritual teacher or guide, often used to respectfully refer to Sree Narayana Narayana Guru.

Humanity is one family: A core teaching of Sree Narayana Guru, emphasizing the inherent equality and interconnectedness of all human beings, transcending artificial divisions.

Inter-caste dining: A radical social reform activity encouraged by Guru and the SNDP Yogam, where people from different castes would eat together, breaking down barriers of untouchability.

Karunagappally: A town in Kerala where Nanu studied under the Sanskrit scholar Komampalli Raman Pillai Asan.

Karuna: Sanskrit term for compassion, empathy, or mercy.

Komampalli Raman Pillai Asan: A renowned Sanskrit scholar under whom Nanu received further education.

Krishnan Vaidyar: Nanu's maternal uncle, an esteemed Ayurvedic physician and Sanskrit scholar, who was a significant influence on his early intellectual development.

Kumaran Asan: One of Sree Narayana Guru's most celebrated disciples, who became a towering figure in Malayalam literature and a leading voice of social change through his poetry.

Kumbham: A Malayalam month, corresponding to February-March, when the Aruvippuram consecration took place.

Lamps: A symbolic object consecrated by Guru in some temples, representing inner wisdom, spiritual light, and awakening.

Lord Krishna: A prominent deity in Hinduism, worshipped as the Supreme Being or as the eighth avatar of Vishnu.

Madan Asan: Nanu's father, a respected village teacher with knowledge of Sanskrit.

Malayalam: The official language of Kerala, Guru's native language.

Maruthwamala: A small, sacred hill near Nagercoil, where Nanu Swami undertook intense meditation and attained enlightenment.

Maulvis: Muslim religious scholars or clerics.

Medicinal plants: Plants with healing properties, often found in traditional Indian medicine (Ayurveda).

Mirrors: A symbolic object consecrated by Guru in some temples, representing the idea that God is within oneself, and one sees the divine when looking into the mirror.

Nanu: The affectionate childhood name for Narayanan, who later became Sree Narayana Guru.

Nanu Asan: The respectful title given to Nanu when he worked as a teacher.

Nanu Swami: The name by which Nanu was known after his spiritual enlightenment and ascetic wanderings.

Nazhika: A traditional unit of distance in Kerala, roughly equivalent to 4 kilometers.

Neyyattinkara: A town in Kerala, a place where Nanu had relatives and often traveled.

One caste, one religion, one God for mankind: A famous and revolutionary maxim by Sree Narayana Guru, advocating for universal brotherhood and the underlying unity of humanity despite diverse expressions of faith.

Organization: A key principle taught by Guru ("Gain strength through organization"), emphasizing collective effort and structured movements for social change.

Paddy fields: Rice fields, a common agricultural landscape in Kerala.

Palanquin: A covered litter, typically for one person, carried by two or more bearers, used for travel in earlier times.

Pancha Suddhi (Five Purities): A holistic concept of purity advocated by Guru for individual life, encompassing physical, food, mental, speech, and action purity.

Parivrajaka: A wandering ascetic or renunciate in Indian spiritual traditions.

Pillathadam: A flat rocky area on the summit of Maruthwamala.

Plato, Descartes, Shankaracharya: Philosophers mentioned in the context of academic knowledge vs. practical wisdom. Plato (ancient Greek), Descartes (French, founder of modern philosophy), Shankaracharya (influential Indian philosopher, proponent of Advaita Vedanta).

Pulaya: A historically marginalized and oppressed Dalit community in Kerala, subjected to severe untouchability.

Puranas: A genre of ancient Hindu sacred texts, containing myths, legends, and genealogies.

Puttu: A popular steamed breakfast dish from Kerala, used by Guru as an analogy for the flaws in the education system.

Religious reform: Guru's efforts to purify and redefine religious practices, challenging superstitions, caste-based exclusion, and divisive interpretations of faith.

Samadhi: A state of intense concentration achieved through meditation; also, the final conscious departure of a saint from the physical body, often signifying liberation.

Sanskrit: An ancient Indo-Aryan language, the primary liturgical language of Hinduism and the language of classical Hindu philosophy.

Sanyasi: A renunciate or ascetic in Hinduism, one who has given up worldly attachments for spiritual pursuit.

Sattvic: Pertaining to 'sattva' (goodness, purity, harmony) in Ayurvedic and Yogic traditions, often used to describe pure and wholesome food.

Self-respect: A core value promoted by Guru to uplift marginalized communities, instilling a sense of dignity and inherent worth.

Shivalinga: An aniconic representation of the Hindu deity Shiva, often worshipped in temples.

Shivaratri: A major Hindu festival celebrated annually in honor of the god Shiva.

Shiva: A principal deity of Hinduism, the Destroyer within the Trimurti (the Hindu trinity).

Sivagiri: The main ashram and spiritual headquarters established by Sree Narayana Guru, located near Varkala.

SNDP Yogam (Sree Narayana Dharma Paripalana Yogam): An influential social and religious organization founded in 1903, directly inspired by Guru's vision, working for the upliftment of marginalized communities in Kerala.

Sree Narayana Guru: The revered spiritual leader, philosopher, and social reformer whose life and mission are the subject of this book. Also known as Narayanan, Nanu, and Nanu Swami.

Sree Narayana Dharma Paripalana Yogams (SNDP Yogams): Refers to the collective local branches and activities of the SNDP Yogam.

Sri Lanka: An island nation south of India, which also saw the spread of Guru's teachings and the SNDP Yogam's influence among the diaspora.

Subrahmanya: A Hindu deity, the son of Shiva and Parvati, worshipped primarily in South India as Murugan or Kartikeya.

Swami: A respectful title for a Hindu ascetic or religious teacher.

Tamil: A Dravidian language spoken predominantly by the Tamil people of India and Sri Lanka.

Temple entry: The right for all castes, particularly historically excluded ones, to enter Hindu temples for worship, a major social reform championed by Guru.

Thirukkural: A classic Tamil text consisting of 1,330 short couplets (kurals), known for its universal ethical and moral teachings. Guru later translated it into Malayalam.

Thiruvananthapuram: The capital city of Kerala, formerly known as Trivandrum.

Thycattu Ayya: A profound master of yoga and spiritual disciplines, under whom Nanu Swami intensely trained.

Unity: A core principle advocated by Guru, emphasizing the strength found in collective action and shared humanity.

Upper-caste: Refers to the traditionally privileged castes in the Hindu social hierarchy, such as Brahmins and Nairs.

Vadavinkode Bhavanam: A house near Aruvippuram where Guru often stayed, which became an informal ashram and center for his teachings.

Varanappally household: The home where Nanu resided while studying under Komampalli Raman Pillai Asan in Karunagappally.

Varkala: A coastal town in Kerala, known for its spiritual significance and home to Sivagiri Ashram.

Vayalvarathu Veedu: Literally "the house beside the paddy fields," Sree Narayana Guru's birthplace in Chempazhanthi.

Vidyarambham: A traditional Hindu ceremony marking the formal initiation of a child into the world of learning, usually at age five.

Yajna: A Hindu ritual of sacrifice, offering, or worship, performed to achieve specific goals or for general well-being. Guru's life was described as a yajna in service of humanity.

Yoga/Yogic disciplines: A system of physical, mental, and spiritual practices originating in ancient India, aimed at achieving union with the divine or self-realization.

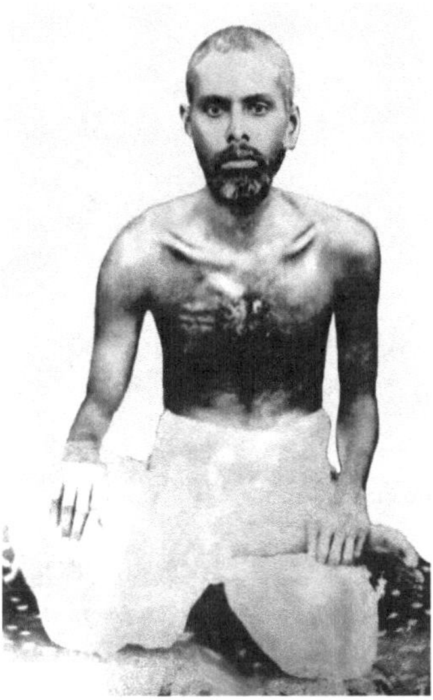

Vayalvaaram Veedu

Vayalvaaram Veedu now

Guru's Sisters

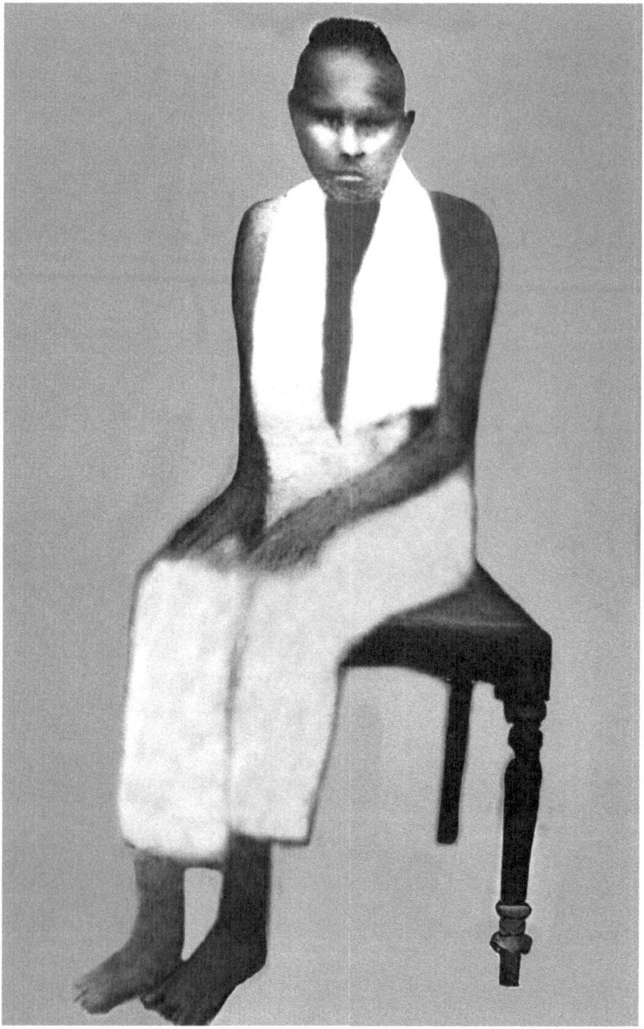

Guru as a teacher at Anchuthengu

Varanapally Tharavaadu

Maruthwamala

Pillathadam, Maruthwamala

Thycattu Ayya Swami

Chattampi Swamikal

Nataraja Guru (Dr P Natarajan)

Ramana Maharshi

Aruvippuram Village

Nanuswamy coming out of the river with Sivalinga (Artists impression)

Aruvippuram Temple (old)

Aruvippuram Temple now

Aruvipuram Madom

Sarvamatha Sammelanam

Formation of Sree Narayana Dharma Sangam

The jack fruit tree, at the shadows of which
SNDP Yogam was born

First AGM of SNDP Yogam

Second AGM of SNDP Yogam

Entrance to Adwaithasram, Aluva

Guru Mandiram at Adwaithasram

Dr. Palpu

Kumaranasan with Guru

Sarada Devi

Sarada Madom Varkala

Guru on his first visit to Mangalore

Guru with Members of Kannur Mahila Samajam

Sreenarayana Guru and Ganghiji

Sreenarayana Guru with Rabindranatha Tagore

Sree Narayana Society, Colombo

Procession by Sree Narayana Society, Colombo

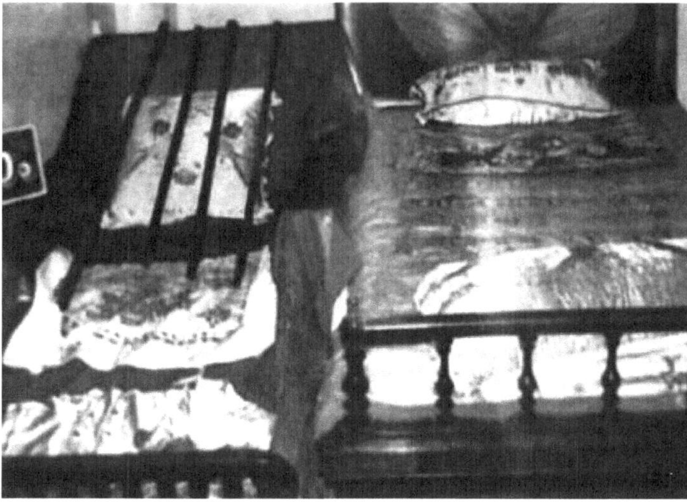

Guru's cot and walking sticks preserved at Vaidika Madom

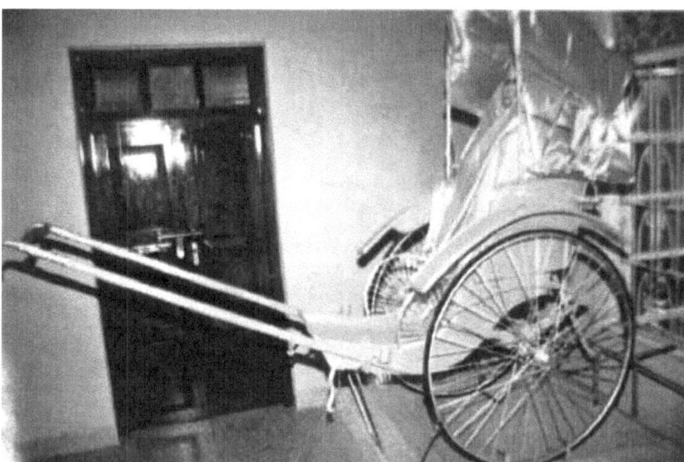

Hand pulled rickshaw used by Sreenarayana Guru

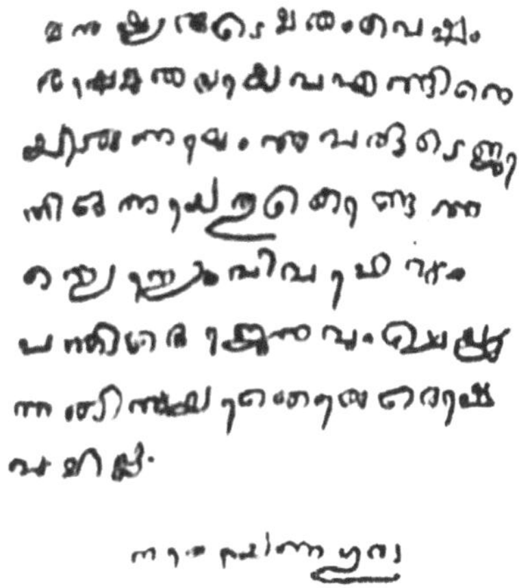

Guru's handwriting

Guru's Samadhi (old picture)

Guru's Samadhi (Now)

15

A Pilgrim's Guide Places, Distances and Getting There

Sivagiri Mutt is a spiritual oasis and pilgrimage center located atop Sivagiri Hill, serving as the samadhi (final resting place) of Sree Narayana Guru. Visitors can explore the peaceful ashram, learn about the Guru's teachings of "One Caste, One Religion, One God," and visit the Sarada Temple dedicated to the Goddess of Knowledge. The Mutt's distinctive multi-tiered white terraces and serene environment are ideal for contemplation. The Guru's birthday (Gurudeva Jayanthi) and Samadhi day, both in August/September, are celebrated with colorful processions, debates, seminars, public meetings, and cultural shows, drawing thousands of followers in yellow attire. Another important festival is the Sivagiri pilgrimage, observed from December 30th to January 1st, when thousands of pilgrims in yellow attire gather from across Kerala at the Guru's Samadhi.

Just a short distance from Sivagiri is **Varkala**, a stunning coastal town known for its unique laterite cliffs and pristine beaches. **Varkala Beach**, also known as **Papanasam Beach**, is famous for its distinct geological formation of red laterite cliffs adjacent to the Arabian Sea. This popular coastal area offers natural beauty, spiritual significance, and recreational activities like swimming, sunbathing, and surfing. It is also a significant site for the **Karkidaka Vavu Bali** ritual, observed on the new moon day in the Malayalam month of Karkkidakam (July-August). During this time, Hindus perform prayers and rituals to appease the departed souls of their ancestors, with hundreds of thousands gathering at Varkala beach.

Towering above Varkala Beach are the dramatic red **Varkala Cliffs,** offering panoramic views of the coastline, especially at sunrise and sunset. The cliff-top promenade features charming cafes, restaurants serving fresh seafood, and shops selling local handicrafts and souvenirs, making it a vibrant hub for relaxation and exploration.

The Janardanaswamy Temple, also known as Varkala Temple, is a renowned Hindu temple in Janardhanapuram dedicated to Lord Vishnu as Janardanaswamy, or Varkaleswara. Thousands of years old, legend states that Sage Narada directed the Devas, cursed by Lord Brahma to suffer as humans, to perform penance at Varkala to regain immortality, thus establishing the temple.

Edava Beach (Edava Vettakkada Beach), near Varkala Beach and Kappil, is a tranquil stretch of sand offering an undisturbed retreat, ideal for those seeking a serene beach experience. Its calm ambiance and secluded allure make it a perfect destination for honeymooners and couples. The beach's beauty lies in its simplicity, with leisurely walks along its shores where rhythmic waves meet black rocks providing a rejuvenating experience. This small, precious gift of nature remains one of the pristine stretches in North Varkala. A fascinating natural wonder nearby is the estuary linking Edava-Nadayara Lake to the Arabian Sea, creating a spectacular sight during the monsoon when the lake waters rush into the sea. This serene environment is perfect for appreciating untouched nature and Varkala's hidden gems.

Beyond the beaches, Varkala and its surroundings offer rich history and nature. **The Asan Memorial** (Asan Smarakam) in Kayikkara is a museum and cultural center dedicated to Malayalam poet Kumaranasan, featuring exhibits of his manuscripts, letters, and photographs, as well as a library and landscaped grounds.

Anjengo Fort (Anchuthengu Fort), located in a small coastal town between the sea and backwaters near Varkala in Thiruvananthapuram District, was the first trade settlement established by the British East India Company in 1684, despite various colonial powers attempting to occupy the area. "Anjengo" was a British mispronunciation of "Anchuthengu". Though small, its historical relevance in Kerala's colonial history and India's maritime trade attracts visitors. Today, Anjengo Fort stands as a well-preserved historical landmark with high laterite walls and bastions, offering panoramic views of the Arabian Sea. Visitors can explore its barracks, storehouses, and chapel, appreciating its colonial-era architecture, with lookout points and entrances on the east and west. Nearby, there are old churches and a cemetery, and its location between a beach and backwaters makes it a popular tourist destination.

Aruvippuram is a popular tourist destination known for the Aruvippuram Shiva Temple established by Sri Narayana Guru. Beyond the temple, attractions include Koduthooki Mala, a rocky hill with a cave where Guru meditated, and the Aruvikkara Dam on the Karamana River, offering scenic views.

For those interested in the life of Sree Narayana Guru, there are five significant places to visit:

Chempazhanthi: The birthplace of Sree Narayana Guru. The nearest airport is Trivandrum International Airport (TRV), approximately 15 km away. The nearest railway station to Chempazhanthi is Kazhakkottam, 3 km away.

Maruthwamala (also known as Marunthuazh Malai): Where Sree Narayana Guru spent time in penance searching for ultimate truth. It is situated on the way to Kanyakumari from Nagercoil. The nearest airport is Trivandrum International Airport (TRV). Several attractions are located near Marudhamalai Hill Temple, including temples, museums, and natural spots. Popular choices include the Perur Pateeswarar Temple, the TNAU Botanical Garden, Kovai Kondattam (a theme park), and the Isha Yoga Center. Additionally, the Gedee Car Museum, Gass Forest Museum, and Siruvani Waterfalls are also worth considering. Other notable temples include Velliangiri Hill Temple and Dhyanalinga Yogic Temple. For nature lovers, Silent Valley National Park is an option. Other museums include the Kasthuri Sreenivasan Art Gallery & Textile Museum. VOC Park & Zoo is also available.

Aruvippuram: Where Sree Narayana Guru installed the first Sivalinga. Trivandrum International Airport (TRV) to Aruvippuram Temple is 29 kilometers. The nearest railway station is Neyyattinkara, 3 km away.

Sivagiri: Where Sree Narayana Guru set up Sarada Madam and his Ashram, spending most of his later life here. Trivandrum International Airport (TRV) to Sivagiri (Varkala) is 40 km. The nearest railway station is Varkala (Sivagiri), 3 km away.

Other notable attractions in and around Thiruvananthapuram include the Neyyar Wildlife Sanctuary, the Padmanabhaswamy Temple, and various beaches like Vettukadu and Shanghumukham. Several other temples like Maheswaram Sri Sivaparvathi Temple and Arulmigu Adikesava Perumal Temple are also located nearby. Other points of interest include Erattinpuram Rocky River View Point, Naanumala Hill, Koyikkal Palace, Freedom Struggle Memorial, Ammavan Para, and Kowdiar Palace.

Kanyakumari, the southernmost tip of mainland India, offers a variety of attractions including Sanguthurai Beach, Thiruvalluvar Statue, Mahatma Gandhi Memorial, Tsunami Memorial Park, Vivekananda Rock Memorial, Sucheendram Temple, Thanumalayan Temple, Lord Subramanya Temple, Courtallam Falls, Chitharal Jain Monuments, and Mathur Aqueduct.

Adwaithasramam in Aluva: This ashram served as Sree Narayana Guru's second home. The nearest airport to Adwaithasramam (Aluva) is Cochin International Airport (COK). The nearest railway station to Adwaithasramam is Aluva railway station. Other attractions nearby include Aluva Palace, Thottakkattukara Sree Krishna Swamy Temple, Marthanda Varma Bridge, Periyar River, and Aluva Manappuram Siva Temple, Aluva.

Kerala is well-connected by road and rail, ensuring easy transport. For local transport, public and private buses, app-based taxi cars, and auto-rickshaws are available.

Tips for visitors include dressing modestly when visiting Sivagiri Mutt and other religious sites by covering shoulders and knees. The best time to visit is from October to March, offering pleasant weather for sightseeing. Visitors are encouraged to embrace local culture by savoring authentic Kerala cuisine, exploring local markets, and experiencing an Ayurvedic massage. A visit to Sivagiri is an invitation to explore its spiritual depths, as well as the natural beauty, rich history, and vibrant culture of the surrounding Varkala region.